MUSEUM ETHICS

A Report to the

AMERICAN ASSOCIATION
OF MUSEUMS

by its

Committee on Ethics

1978

This report was first published in the March/April 1978 issue of MUSEUM NEWS, the journal of the American Association of Museums.

American Association of Museums
1055 Thomas Jefferson St., N.W.
Washington, D.C. 20007
(202) 338-5300

Contents

Preface

S ince the publication of the last Code of Ethics by the American Association of Museums in 1925, our museums have expanded their activities into disciplines and activities seldom a part of their institutional ancestors. Educational outreach, historical, environmental assessment and a host of other programs have become a normal and respected part of museum activity. Simultaneously, museum policy with respect to collecting has been influenced by expanded public awareness, a changing social conscience, and the decrease in intellectual isolationism and specialization among museum professionals. These expansive changes have caused the profession, one in which ethical requirements above and beyond the legal are everywhere apparent, to reexamine the ethical basis of its operational decisions. Some within the profession ask how their own views, or those of others, compare with the consensus or, for that matter, whether a consensus exists. Others question the ethical propriety of acts observed within their own institutions or others.

These thoughts were brought to the officers and council of the American Association of Museums during the mid-1970s. At the national meeting of the association in Fort Worth in 1974 President Joseph M. Chamberlain appointed a Committee on Ethics, which was continued in expanded form by his successor as AAM president, Joseph Veach Noble. This committee was to identify the ethical principles underlying museum operations in the broadest sense as viewed by the profession at this point in history.

The committee members were appointed by the president of the association in consultation with the committee chairman. Those sections of the document that discuss museum governance were prepared in conjunction with the Trustee Ethics Subcommittee, appointed in part by the Trustees Committee of the association. The members of the Trustee Ethics Subcommittee were subsequently added to the Committee on Ethics.

Funds enabling the committee to meet were provided in part by the National Museum Act administered by the Smithsonian Institution, and by the Rockefeller Brothers Fund, support gratefully acknowledged here. The chairman also acknowledges with sincere appreciation the contributions made by each member of the committee, and the institution of each for its enabling indirect support of this effort.

The following serve as members of the Committee on Ethics:

WILLIAM T. ALDERSON, *Director, American Association for State and Local History*, Nashville, Tennessee

EDWARD P. ALEXANDER, *Director of Museum Studies, The University of Delaware*, Newark, Delaware

ROBERT G. BAKER, *Chief Curator, Arizona State Museum*, Tucson, Arizona

MICHAEL BOTWINICK, *Director, The Brooklyn Museum*, Brooklyn, New York

G. ELLIS BURCAW, *Director, University of Idaho Museum*, Moscow, Idaho

CHARLES C. CUNNINGHAM, JR., *Trustee, Museum of Fine Arts*, Boston, Massachusetts

WILLIAM A. FAGALY, *Chief Curator, New Orleans Museum of Art*, New Orleans, Louisiana

PEGGY LOAR, *Program Director, Institute of Museum Services*, Washington, D.C.

GILES W. MEAD, *Director, The Natural History Museum of Los Angeles County*, Los Angeles, California

THOMAS MESSER, *Director, The Solomon R. Guggenheim Museum*, New York, New York

ELLEN M. MYETTE, *Assistant Curator, Renwick Gallery, National Collection of Fine Arts, Smithsonian Institution*, Washington, D.C.

BARBARA Y. NEWSOM, *Staff Associate, The Rockefeller Brothers Fund*, New York, New York

MILTON F. PERRY, *Director of History, Historic Kansas City Foundation*, Kansas City, Missouri

JEROME G. ROZEN, JR., *Deputy Director for Research, The American Museum of Natural History*, New York, New York

FRANKLIN G. SMITH, *Superintendent, Chamizal National Memorial*, El Paso, Texas

MICHAEL SPOCK, *Director, The Children's Museum*, Boston, Massachusetts

SUSAN STITT, *Director, The Museums at Stony Brook*, Stony Brook, New York

WILLIAM G. SWARTCHILD, JR., *Chairman of the Board of Trustees, Field Museum of Natural History*, Chicago, Illinois

H. J. SWINNEY, *Director, The Margaret Woodbury Strong Museum*, Rochester, New York

ALAN D. ULLBERG, *Associate General Counsel, Smithsonian Institution*, Washington, D.C.

DRAFTING COMMITTEE: EDWARD P. ALEXANDER, MICHAEL BOTWINICK, GILES W. MEAD and ALAN D. ULLBERG

TECHNICAL EDITOR: ALAN D. ULLBERG

CHAIRMAN: GILES W. MEAD

On matters of both substance and wording, the committee members were in total accord on few if any issues. Each, accepting compromise, has endorsed the final draft.

The committee has not been charged with the implementation of its report. It is presented here as a report to the association by its Committee on Ethics. The members of the committee hope that the association, its officers, council and membership will use this report toward the betterment of our museums and the furtherance of their purposes.

GILES W. MEAD

March 1978

MUSEUM
ETHICS

Introduction

Our museums include a broad array of diverse institutions that have come to be an important part of the intellectual and emotional life of man. Most of them have as their primary attribute a collection of tangible objects which they care for and hold in trust for the benefit and use of mankind, present and future. In all other respects, these institutions are as diverse as the intellects that conceived them and those that provide their current direction.

This report presents certain statements related to ethical conduct that, in the committee's opinion, represent the consensus of the profession. The committee has concluded that its primary role is to focus the attention of the profession on these ethical issues, but it recognizes the danger of oversimplified strictures. Whenever possible it has chosen to define its sense of the ethical issue and to provide statements of the consensus of the profession regarding beliefs and attitudes for the guidance of the conscientious individual faced with his* personal or institutional problems.

This report does not pretend to completeness. The many disciplines and professions that cluster around the museum as an entity may find it not specific enough. Further statements of ethical or operational principles suited to specific needs are called for. Institutions distant from the classical concept, for example zoos and aquariums, may find major issues that are central to them omitted.

This report on ethical conduct presumes the acknowledged existence of a more fundamental code that is the foundation of civilized society. It is not intended to be a policy or procedural outline for museum administration or governance. To deal with the issues raised, each institution should develop its own document. Each individual can use the guidelines suggested in this report to focus his attention on these crucial issues. The choice of content reflects the committee's understanding of museum history and current practice. Therefore the statements are intended to be guidelines against which current museum policy and practice can be tested for ethical content. Little of the report is amenable to literal or absolute interpretation, and the force and intonation

*In the text of this statement, "he" and related pronouns are used in the classical sense to denote the person, male or female.

of much that is included will differ among museums and with the passage of time.

The separate sections of this report do not define the extent to which ethical standards apply to others beyond individual museum employees, volunteers and trustees. This statement must be understood to apply to the activities of third persons when they or their actions are relevant to the museum. Such persons may include members of the museum person's own household, his close relatives or friends, or other associates. It is not the precise degree of relationship that governs applicability of ethical standards, but rather the facts of the relationship. The museum person is ethically obligated to ensure that the principles of this code are not violated on his behalf by the acts of others, and to ensure, as far as possible, that the acts of others do not place the employee or his institution in a position of compromise or embarrassment.

The Collection

Management, Maintenance and Conservation

Museums generally derive most of their prominence and importance from their collections, and these holdings constitute the primary difference between museums and other kinds of institutions. The collections, whether works of art, artifacts or specimens from the natural world, are an essential part of the collective cultural fabric, and each museum's obligation to its collection is paramount.

Each object is an integral part of a cultural or scientific composite. That context also includes a body of information about the object which establishes its proper place and importance and without which the value of the object is diminished. The maintenance of this information in orderly and retrievable form is critical to the collection and is a central obligation of those charged with collection management.

An ethical duty of museums is to transfer to our successors, when possible in enhanced form, the material record of human culture and the natural world. They must be in control of their collections and know the location and the condition of the objects that they hold. Procedures must be established for the periodic evaluation of the condition of the collections and for their general and special maintenance.

The physical care of the collection and its accessibility must be in keeping with professionally accepted standards. Failing this, museum governance and management are ethically obliged either to effect correction of the deficiency or to dispose of the collection, preferably to another institution.

Acquisition and Disposal

No collection exists in isolation. Its course generally will be influenced by changes in cultural, scholarly or educational trends, strengths and specializations developing in other institutions, policy and law regarding the traffic in various kinds of objects, the status of plant and animal populations, and the desire to improve the collection.

In the delicate area of acquisition and disposal of museum objects, the museum must weigh carefully the interests of the public for which

11

it holds the collection in trust, the donor's intent in the broadest sense, the interests of the scholarly and the cultural community, and the institution's own financial well-being.

Every institution should develop and make public a statement of its policy regarding the acquisition and disposal of objects. Objects collected by the museum should be relevant to its purposes and activities, be accompanied by a valid legal title, preferably be unrestricted but with any limitations clearly described in an instrument of conveyance, and be properly cataloged, conserved, stored or exhibited. Museums must remain free to improve their collections through selective disposal and acquisition and intentionally to sacrifice specimens for well-considered analytical, educational or other purposes. In general objects should be kept as long as they retain their physical integrity, authenticity and usefulness for the museum's purposes.

Illicit trade in objects encourages the destruction of sites, the violation of national exportation laws, and contravention of the spirit of national patrimony. Museums must acknowledge the relationship between the marketplace and the initial and often destructive taking of an object for the commercial market. They must not support that illicit market. Each museum must develop a method for considering objects of this status for acquisition that will allow it to acquire or accept an object only when it can determine with reasonable certainty that it has not been immediately derived from this illicit trade and that its acquisition does not contribute to the continuation of that trade.

Basic to the existence of institutions devoted to natural history is the obligation to acquire, preserve and use representative samples of the earth's biota, living and extinct. Museums should assume a position of leadership in the effort to halt the continuing degradation of our natural history resources. Each institution must develop policies that allow it to conduct its activities within the complexities of existing legislation and with the reasonable certainty that its approach is consistent with the spirit and intent of these programs.

Institutions and their staffs should be encouraged to anticipate the possible consequences of their own actions as they pertain to the acquisition of plants and animals. They must be aware of the potential damage that such acquisitions might have on the population of a species, a community of organisms or the environment in general. They must conduct their collecting activities within recognized standards that avoid insofar as possible the adverse effects of such activities. These principles apply to the acquisition of objects for all museum activities including educational, scholarly, commercial or display purposes.

When disposing of an object, the museum must determine that it has the legal right to do so. When mandatory restrictions accompany the acquisition they must be observed unless it can be clearly shown that adherence to such restrictions is impossible or substantially detrimental to the institution. A museum can only be relieved from such restrictions by an appropriate legal procedure. When precatory statements accompany the acquisition, they must be carefully considered, and consultation with the donor or his heirs should be attempted.

The museum must not allow objects from its collections to be acquired privately by any museum employee, officer, volunteer, member of its governing board or his representative, unless they are sold publicly and with the complete disclosure of their history. Objects, materials or supplies of trifling value which the museum cannot sell and that must be discarded may be given to anyone associated with the institution or to the public.

In disposing of an object, due consideration must be given the museum community in general as well as the wishes and financial needs of the institution. Sales to, or exchanges between, institutions should be considered as well as disposal through the trade. In addition to the financial return from disposals, the museum should consider the full range of factors affecting the public interest.

While the governing entity bears final responsibility for the collection including both the acquisition and disposal process, the curatorial and administrative staff together with their technical associates are best qualified to assess the pertinence of an object to the collection or the museum's programs. Only for clear and compelling reasons should an object be disposed of against the advice of the museum's professional staff.

Appraisals

Performing appraisals or authentications can be useful to a museum and the public it serves; however, there should be institutional policy covering the circumstances where appraisals are desirable or permissible as an official museum-related function. Any appraisal or authentication must represent an honest and objective judgment, and must include an indication of how the determination was made.

Commercial Use

In arranging for the manufacture and sale of replicas, reproductions or other commercial items adapted from an object in a museum's collection, all aspects of the commercial venture must be carried out in a manner that will not discredit either the integrity of the museum or the intrinsic value of the original object. Great care must be taken to identify permanently such objects for what they are, and to ensure the accuracy and high quality of their manufacture.

Availability of Collections

Although the public must have reasonable access to the collections on a nondiscriminatory basis, museums assume as a primary responsibility the safeguarding of their materials and therefore may regulate access to them. Some parts of the collections may be set aside for the active scholarly pursuits of staff members, but normally only for the duration of an active research effort.

When a staff member involved in scholarly research moves to another institution, the museum should give special consideration to the need he may have of objects or materials that remain in the collections. Such needs should be accommodated, where possible, by loans to the staff member's present institution.

The judgment and recommendation of professional staff members regarding the use of the collections must be given utmost consideration. In formulating his recommendation the staff member must let his judgment be guided by two primary objectives: the continued physical integrity and safety of the object or collection, and high scholarly or educational purposes.

Truth in Presentation

Within the museum's primary charge, the preservation of significant materials unimpaired for the future, is the responsibility of museum professionals to use museum collections for the creation and dissemination of new knowledge. Intellectual honesty and objectivity in the presentation of objects is the duty of every professional. The stated origin of the object or attribution of work must reflect the thorough and honest investigation of the curator and must yield promptly to change with the advent of new fact or analysis.

Museums may address a wide variety of social, political, artistic or scientific issues. Any can be appropriate, if approached objectively and without prejudice.

The museum professional must use his best effort to ensure that exhibits are honest and objective expressions and do not perpetuate myths or stereotypes. Exhibits must provide with candor and tact an honest and meaningful view of the subject. Sensitive areas such as ethnic and social history are of most critical concern.

The research and preparation of an exhibition will often lead the professional to develop a point of view or interpretive sense of the

14

material. He must clearly understand the point where sound professional judgment ends and personal bias begins. He must be confident that the resultant presentation is the product of objective judgment.

Human Remains and Sacred Objects

Research, which provides the very basic foundation for knowledge, is a dynamic and therefore continuing process. It is essential that collections of human remains and sacred objects upon which research is based not be arbitrarily restricted, be securely housed and carefully maintained as archival collections in scholarly institutions, and always be available to qualified researchers and educators, but not to the morbidly curious.

We have learned much about human development and cultural history from human burials and sacred objects. There is merit in continuing such investigations. But if we are to maintain an honorable position as humanists concerned with the worth of the individual, the study of skeletal material and sacred objects must be achieved with dignity. Research on such objects and their housing and care must be accomplished in a manner acceptable not only to fellow professionals but to those of various beliefs.

Although it is occasionally necessary to use skeletal and other sensitive material in interpretive exhibits, this must be done with tact and with respect for the feelings for human dignity held by all peoples. Such an exhibit exists to convey to the visitor an understanding of the lives of those who lived or live under very different circumstances. These materials must not be used for other more base purposes.

The Staff

General Deportment

Employment by a museum, whether privately or governmentally supported, is a public trust involving great responsibility. In all activities museum employees must act with integrity and in accordance with the most stringent ethical principles as well as the highest standards of objectivity.

Every museum employee is entitled to a measure of personal independence equal to that granted comparable professionals in other disciplines, consistent with his professional and staff responsibilities. While loyalty to the museum must be paramount, the employee also has the right to a private life independent of the institution. But museums enjoy high public visibility and their employees a generous measure of public esteem. To the public the museum employee is never wholly separable from his institution. He can never consider himself or his activities totally independent of his museum despite disclaimers that he may offer. Any museum-related action by the individual may reflect on the institution or be attributed to it. He must be concerned not only with the true personal motivations and interests as he sees them but also the way in which such actions might be construed by the outside observer.

Conflict of Interest

Museum employees should never abuse their official positions or their contacts within the museum community, impair in any way the performance of their official duties, compete with their institutions, or bring discredit or embarrassment to any museum or to the profession in any activity, museum related or not. They should be prepared to accept as conditions of employment the restrictions that are necessary to maintain public confidence in museums and in the museum profession.

To protect the institution and provide guidance to its employees, each museum should issue a comprehensive and well-understood policy covering ethical questions related to personal activities and conflicts of interest. That statement must define the procedures essential to the implementation of and compliance with stated policy.

17

Responsibilities to the Collections and Other Museum Property

Museum employees should not acquire objects from the collections owned or controlled by their museums unless such transactions have been subjected to a formal disclosure procedure by the individual and the institution, and were available through a disposal process totally public in nature.

No staff member should use in his home or for any other personal purpose any object or item that is a part of the museum's collections or under the guardianship of the museum, or use any other property, supplies or resources of the museum except for the official business of the institution. To the extent that factual circumstances or special policies warrant exceptions to this principle, the circumstances or policies should be a matter of written record.

The reputation and name of a museum are valuable assets and should not be exploited either for personal advantage or the advantage of any other person or entity.

Information about the administrative and nonscholarly activities of the institution that an employee may acquire in the course of his duties, and that is not generally known or available to the public, must be treated as information proprietary to the museum. Such information should not be used for personal advantage or other purposes detrimental to the institution.

Staff members should be circumspect in referring members of the public to outside suppliers of services such as appraisers or restorers. Whenever possible, more than a single qualified source should be provided so that no appearance of personal favoritism in referrals is created.

Personal Collecting

The acquiring, collecting and owning of objects is not in itself unethical, and can enhance professional knowledge and judgment. However, the acquisition, maintenance and management of a personal collection by a museum employee can create ethical questions. Extreme care is required whenever an employee collects objects similar to those collected by his museum, and some museums may choose to restrict or prohibit personal collecting. In any event, the policies covering personal collecting should be included in the policy statements of each museum and communicated to its staff.

No employee may compete with his institution in any personal collecting activity. The museum must have the right, for a specified and limited period, to acquire any object purchased or collected by any staff member at the price paid by the employee.

Museum employees must inform the appropriate officials about all personal acquisitions. They also must disclose all circumstances regarding personal collections and collecting activities, and furnish in a timely manner information on prospective sales or exchanges.

A museum's policy on personal collecting should specify what kind of objects staff members are permitted or not permitted to acquire, what manner of acquisition is permissible and whether different types of employees have different rights. Policy should specify the method of disclosure required for the staff member. It also should specify the manner and time period within which the museum can exercise the rights it has to purchase objects staff members have acquired for their personal collections. Such a policy can be most effective if explicitly a part of the conditions of employment clearly understood by all employees.

Except by special agreement with individual staff members, the right of a museum to acquire from employees objects collected personally should not extend to objects that were collected prior to the staff member's employment by that museum. Objects that are bequests or genuine personal gifts should be exempt from the museum's right to acquire.

No museum employee may use his museum affiliation to promote his or any associate's personal collecting activities. No employee may participate in any dealing (buying and selling for profit as distinguished from occasional sale or exchange from a personal collection) in objects similar or related to the objects collected by the museum. Dealing by employees in objects that are collected by any other museum can present serious problems. It should be permitted only after full disclosure, review and approval by the appropriate museum official.

Outside Employment and Consulting

Certain types of outside employment, including self-employment and paid consulting activities, can be of benefit to both the institution and the employee by stimulating personal professional development. Remuneration may be monetary or nonmonetary, direct or indirect.

All employment activity must be undertaken within the fundamental premise that the employee's primary responsibility is to his institution; that the activity will not interfere with his ability to discharge this responsibility; and that it will not compromise the professional integrity of the employee or the reputation of the museum.

Museum employees often will be considered representatives of their institutions while they are engaged in activities or duties similar to those they perform for their museum, even though their work may be wholly independent of the institution. In other instances an employee's duties within or outside the institution may require little specialized knowledge of the functioning of a museum. In either case employees must disclose to the director or other appropriate superior the facts concerning any planned outside employment or consulting arrangements that are in any way related to the functions that such employees perform for their museums. Disclosure should not be required for small businesses or similar activities that are entirely unrelated to the work the individual carries out for his institution.

Appraisals, as an official museum activity and subject to well-defined policy, can be useful to a museum and its constituency. As an outside activity of an individual staff member it can present serious problems. No staff member should appraise without the express approval of the director. The related areas of identification, authentication and description, when pursued as an outside activity, should be subject to clearly defined museum policy.

The name of and the employee's connection with the museum should be sparingly and respectfully used in connection with outside activities.

In deference to the constitutional rights of museum employees to freedom of speech and association, disclosure should not be required for their activities on behalf of voluntary community groups or other public service organizations, except for those organizations such as other museums where the staff member could appear to be acting in his official capacity. Museum professionals should conduct themselves so that their activities on behalf of community or public service organizations do not reflect adversely on the reputation or integrity of their museum.

Gifts, Favors, Discounts and Dispensations

Museum employees and others in a close relationship to them must not accept gifts, favors, loans or other dispensations or things of value that are available to them in connection with their duties for the institution. Gifts include discounts on personal purchases from suppliers who sell items or furnish services to the museum, except where such discounts regularly are offered to the general public. Gifts also can include offers of outside employment or other advantageous arrangements for the museum employee or another person or entity. Salaries together with related benefits should be considered complete remuneration for all museum-related activities.

Employees should be permitted to retain gifts of trifling value when acceptance would not appear to impair their judgment or otherwise influence decisions. Meals, accommodations and travel services while on official business may be accepted if clearly in the interest of the museum.

Museum employees have the right to accept and retain gifts that originate from purely personal or family relationships. It must be recognized that genuine personal gifts may originate from individuals who have a potentially beneficial relationship with the museum. In such cases the staff member is obliged to protect both himself and his institution by fully disclosing the circumstances to the appropriate museum official.

Teaching, Lecturing, Writing and Other Creative Activities

Museum staff personnel should be encouraged to teach, lecture and write, as desirable activities that aid professional development. Museums should facilitate such activities so long as there is not undue interference with performance of regular duties, and employees do not take advantage of their museum positions for personal monetary gain or appear to compromise the integrity of their institution.

The employee must recognize that when an outside activity is directly related to his regular duties for the institution he is obliged to reach an agreement with the institution concerning all aspects of that activity.

Employees should obtain the approval of the institution of plans for any significant amount of outside teaching, lecturing, writing or editing. Any contemplated uses of the museum's research facilities, staff assistance and property such as copying machines, slides or objects from the collections should be described, and approvals should be obtained for uses of museum property in connection with such outside efforts.

The proprietary interest of both museum and individual in copyrights, royalties and similar properties should be a part of stated general institutional policy supplemented, through mutual agreement, to conform to the needs of the specific project.

Museum employees who are creative artists or pursue similar outside interests must perform these activities in such a way that their status with the institution is not compromised and the institution not embarrassed. It must be recognized that the exhibition of objects in a museum can enhance their value, and museums should display materials created by staff members only under circumstances in which objectivity in their selection can be clearly demonstrated.

Field Study and Collecting

Field exploration, collecting and excavating by museum workers present ethical problems that are both complex and critical. Such efforts, especially in other countries, present situations that can result in difficult interpersonal and international problems. The statements that follow are offered with the knowledge that any action also must be guided by good judgment, tasteful deportment and current knowledge.

Any field program must be preceded by investigation, disclosure and communication sufficient to ascertain that the activity is legal; is pursued with the full knowledge, approval, and when applicable the collaboration of all individuals and entities to whom the activity is appropriately of concern; and is conducted for scholarly or educational purposes. A general if not specific statement of the nature of the objects to be collected, the purposes that they are intended to serve and their final disposition must be prepared and should be fully understood by all affected parties.

Any field program must be executed in such a way that all participants act legally and responsibly in acquiring specimens and data; that they discourage by all practical means unethical, illegal and destructive practices associated with acquiring, transporting and importing objects; and that they avoid, insofar as possible, even the appearance of engaging in clandestine activity, be it museum-related or not. Normally no material should be acquired that cannot be properly cared for and used.

In both act and appearance participants must honor the beliefs and customs of host individuals and societies. General deportment must be such that future field work at the site or in the area will not be jeopardized.

On completion of field work, full and prompt reporting of the activity should be made to all appropriate parties; all precatory and mandatory agreements must be fulfilled or the failure to do so fully explained; and all material and data collected must be made available to the scholarly community as soon as possible. Materials incorporated into permanent collections should be treated in a manner consistent with recommendations and restrictions developed for their care and use by zoologists, botanists, archeologists, paleontologists or other discipline-specific groups.

22

Museum Management Policy

Professionalism

Members of the museum's administration and governing entities must respect the professional expertise of the staff, each having been engaged because of his special knowledge or ability in some aspect of museum activity. Museum governance must be structured so that the resolution of issues involving professional matters incorporates opinions and professional judgments of relevant members of the museum staff. Responsibility for the final decisions will normally rest with the museum administration and all employees are expected to support these decisions; but no staff member can be required to reverse, alter or suppress his professional judgment in order to conform to a management decision.

Collectively, the staff professionals are most familiar with the museum, its assets and its constituency. As such they should be heard by museum management and governance on matters affecting the general long-term direction of the institution.

Personnel Practices and Equal Opportunity

In all matters related to staffing practices, the standard should be ability in the relevant discipline. In these matters, as well as trustee selection, management practices, volunteer opportunity, collection usage and relationship with the public at large, decisions cannot be made on the basis of discriminatory factors such as race, creed, sex, age, handicap or personal orientation.

It must be remembered that the components of contemporary culture vary by reason of ancestry, experience, education and ability in the extent to which they can share in the museum experience, either as visitors or as a paid or volunteer participant. The museum must recog-

23

nize that it is a significant force within its own social fabric and that these differences do exist. It should seize and indeed create opportunities whenever possible to encourage employment opportunity and the accessibility of the institution as a resource to all people.

Volunteers

Volunteer participation is a strong American tradition, and many museums could not exist without the contributions and personal involvement of devoted volunteers. Where volunteer programs exist, the paid staff should be supportive of volunteers, receive them as fellow workers, and willingly provide appropriate training and opportunity for their intellectual enrichment. While volunteers participate in most museum activities, those with access to the museum's collections, programs and associated privileged information work in areas that are particularly sensitive.

Access to the museum's inner activities is a privilege, and the lack of material compensation for effort expended in behalf of the museum in no way frees the volunteer from adherence to the standards that apply to paid staff. The volunteer must work toward the betterment of the institution and not for personal gain other than the natural gratification and enrichment inherent in museum participation.

Although the museum may accord special privileges, volunteers should not accept gifts, favors, discounts, loans, other dispensations or things of value that accrue to them from other parties in connection with carrying out duties for the institution. Conflict of interest restrictions placed upon the staff must be explained to volunteers and, where relevant, observed by them. Volunteers must hold confidential matters of program function and administration.

Volunteer organizations should understand clearly the policies and programs adopted by museum trustees and not interfere with the administrative application of these policies and programs.

Interpersonal Relationships

The professional museum worker always must be dedicated to the high standards and discipline of his profession, but he also must remain mindful that he is an employee as well as an independent expert. While he must strive for professional excellence in his own specialty, he must simultaneously relate productively to his colleagues, associates and fellow employees. The wisdom and experience of a professional can be lost to the institution if they are not made to act constructively within the total context of the institution.

Interinstitutional Cooperation

If museums intend to contribute to the preservation of humanity's cultural and scientific heritage and the increase of knowledge, each should respond to any opportunity for cooperative action with a similar organization to further these goals. A museum should welcome such cooperative action even if the short-term advantages are few and it will not significantly increase the individual institution's own holdings or enhance its image.

Ownership of Scholarly Material

The object, its documentation and all additional documentation accrued or developed subsequent to its acquisition are the property of the institution.

The analysis of an object for scholarly purposes usually includes the production of interpretive notes, outlines and illustrative material. It can be held that such material is essentially an extension of the intellect and the memory of the scholar, and that as such it is the property of the individual. An equally persuasive case can be made for institutional ownership of all such interpretive material, especially if a staff member was paid to render scholarly analysis. Either is ethically acceptable if the institutional policy is made known beforehand to the staff member, and if the administrative determination of ownership and access is not the result of vindictive or punitive motivation. The guiding ethical principle must be the most effective and timely dissemination of analytical information derived from the collection.

Museum Governance

General Responsibility

The governing body of a museum, usually a board of trustees, serves the public interest as it relates to the museum, and must consider itself accountable to the public as well as to the institution. In most cases the board acts as the ultimate legal entity for the museum, and stands responsible for the formulation and maintenance of its general policies, standards, condition and operational continuity.

Trustees must be unequivocally loyal to the purposes of the museum. Each must understand and respect the basic documents that provide for its establishment, character and governance such as the charter, constitution, bylaws and adopted policies.

Each trustee must devote time and attention to the affairs of the institution and ensure that the museum and its governing board act in accordance with the basic documents and with applicable state and federal laws. In establishing policies or authorizing or permitting activities, trustees especially must ensure that no policies or activities jeopardize the basic nonprofit status of the museum or reflect unfavorably upon it as an institution devoted to public service.

Trustees should not attempt to act in their individual capacities. All actions should be taken as a board, committee or subcommittee, or otherwise in conformance with the bylaws or applicable resolutions. A trustee must work for the institution as a whole, and not act solely as an advocate for particular activities or subunits of the museum.

Trustees should maintain in confidence information learned during the course of their museum activities when that information concerns the administration or activities of the museum and is not generally available to the public. This principle does not preclude public disclosure of information that is properly in the public domain, or information that should be released in fulfilling the institution's accountability to the public.

The governing board holds the ultimate fiduciary responsibility for the museum and for the protection and nurturing of its various assets:

the collections and related documentation, the plant, financial assets and the staff. It is obliged to develop and define the purposes and related policies of the institution, and to ensure that all of the museum's assets are properly and effectively used for public purposes. The board should provide adequate financial protection for all museum officials including themselves, staff and volunteers so that no one will incur inequitable financial sacrifice or legal liabilities arising from the performance of duties for the museum.

The board has especially strong obligations to provide the proper environment for the physical security and preservation of the collections, and to monitor and develop the financial structure of the museum so that it continues to exist as an institution of vitality and quality.

A critical responsibility of the governing board derives from its relationship to the director, the institution's chief executive. The selection of that executive and the continuing surveillance of his activities are primary board responsibilities which cannot be delegated and must be diligently and thoughtfully fulfilled.

In carrying out the duty to the collections, a policy must be developed and adopted by the board governing use of the collections, including acquisitions, loans and the disposal of objects. In formulating policies covering the acceptance of objects or other materials as gifts or loans, the governing board must ensure that the museum understands and respects the restrictions, conditions and all other circumstances associated with gifts and loans.

Conflict of Interest

Individuals who are experienced and knowledgeable in various fields of endeavor related to museum activities can be of great assistance to museums, but conflicts of interest or the appearance of such conflicts may arise because of these interests or activities. Guidelines for the protection of both individual and institution should be established by the governing board of every museum.

The museum trustee must endeavor to conduct all of his activities, including those relating to persons closely associated with him and to business or other organizations, in such a way that no conflict will arise between the other interests and the policies, operations or interests of the museum. The appearance of such conflicts also should be avoided. The reputation of the museum can be damaged should a trustee continue an inappropriate activity concurrent with his service in a position of institutional and public trust.

A procedure minimizing the vulnerability to individual or institutional embarrassment should be formulated and stated by every museum board. Every museum trustee should file with the board a statement disclosing his personal, business or organizational interests and affiliations and those of persons close to him which could be construed as being museum related. Such a statement should include positions as an officer or director as well as relationships to other organizations, if the purposes or programs are in any manner related to or impinge upon the purposes, programs or activities of the museum. Such statements should be made available to the board prior to the trustee's election to that body. As an aid to preparing such statements trustees should be provided relevant data on the museum's operations. Disclosure statements should be updated periodically or whenever significant changes occur.

A visible area for charges of self-interest at the expense of the institution, and of personal use of privileged information, arises whenever a trustee, a member of his family or a close associate personally collects objects of a type collected by the museum. Every museum governing board must clearly state its policy regarding such personal collections. The policy should contain statements to ensure that no trustee competes with the museum for objects; that no trustee takes personal advantage of information available to him because of his board membership; and that should conflict develop between the needs of the individual and the museum, those of the museum will prevail.

No trustee, person close to him, or individual who might act for him may acquire objects from the collections of the museum, except when the object and its source have been advertised, its full history made available, and it is sold at public auction or otherwise clearly offered for sale in the public marketplace.

When museum trustees seek staff assistance for personal needs they should not expect that such help will be rendered to an extent greater than that available to a member of the general public in similar circumstances or with similar needs.

Whenever a matter arises for action by the board, or the museum engages in an activity where there is a possible conflict or the appearance of conflict between the interests of the museum and an outside or personal interest of a trustee or that of a person close to him, the outside interest of the trustee should be made a matter of record. In those cases where the trustee is present when a vote is taken in connection with such a question, he should abstain. In some circumstances he should avoid discussing any planned actions, formally or informally, from which he might appear to benefit. Sometimes neither disclosure nor abstention is sufficient, and the only appropriate solution is resignation.

A museum trustee should not take advantage of information he receives during his service to the institution if his personal use of such information could be financially detrimental to the museum. Any such actions that might impair the reputation of the museum also must be avoided. When a trustee obtains information that could benefit him personally, he should refrain from acting upon it until all issues have been reviewed by an appropriate representative of the museum.

Trustees serve the museum and its public. They should not attempt to derive any personal material advantages from their connection with the institution. Trustees should use museum property only for official purposes, and make no personal use of the museum's collection, property or services in a manner not available to a comparable member of the general public. While loans of objects by trustees can be of great benefit to the museum, it should be recognized that exhibition can enhance the value of the exhibited object. Each museum should adopt a policy concerning the display of objects owned or created by the trustees or staff or in which the trustees or any person close to them have any interests.

The Trustee-Director Relationship

Trustees have an obligation to define the rights, powers and duties of the director. They should work with the director, who is their chief executive officer, in all administative matters, and deal with him openly and with candor. They should avoid giving directions to, acting on behalf of, communicating directly with, or soliciting administrative information from staff personnel, unless such actions are in accord with established procedure or the director is apprised. Staff members should communicate with trustees through the director or with his knowledge, but a procedure should be provided to allow staff personnel to bring grievances directly to the trustees.

The trustees must act as a full board in appointing or dismissing a director, and the relationship between director and board must reflect the primacy of institutional goals over all personal or interpersonal considerations. The director should attend all board meetings and important committee meetings except executive sessions concerning him.

The director has an obligation to provide the trustees with current and complete financial information in comprehensible form; to bring before the board any matters involving policy questions not already determined; and to keep them informed on a timely basis about all other significant or substantial matters, or intended actions affecting the institution.

The director must carry out the policies established by the trustees, and adhere to the budget approved by the board. Whenever it is necessary to deviate from established policies or to alter or exceed budget guidelines, the director should notify the board in advance and request appropriate approval.